wise words

wise words

inspiring lessons about life

www.youaretheauthor.com

First published in the UK in 2002 exclusively for
WHSmith Limited
Greenbridge Road
Swindon SN3 3LD
www.WHSmith.co.uk
by Tangent Publications, an imprint of
Axis Publishing Limited.

Conceived and created by
Axis Publishing Limited
8c Accommodation Road
London NW11 8ED
www.axispublishing.co.uk

Creative Director : Siân Keogh
Managing Editor: Brian Burns
Production Manager: Tim Clarke

ISBN 0–9543620–0–1
4 6 8 10 9 7 5 3

Printed and bound in China

about this book

Wise Words brings together an inspirational selection of powerful and life-affirming phrases that have in one way or another helped people to live their lives, and combines them with evocative and gently amusing animal photographs that bring out the full humour and pathos of the human condition.

We all get upset by life's irritations at some point and lose our motivation, temper or sense of humour (sometimes all three at once!). These inspiring examples of wit and wisdom, written by real people based on their real-life experiences, enable us to regain our sense of perspective and rediscover our love of life. As one of the entries so aptly puts it – every moment in time contains the seeds of happiness.

So don't waste a moment!

about the author

Why have one author when you can have the world? This book has been
compiled using the incredible resource that is the world wide web. From the
many hundreds of contributions that were sent to our website,
www.youaretheauthor.com, we have selected the ones that best sum up what
life is all about – our relationships, our ambitions and our personal well-being.

Please continue to send in your special views, feelings and advice about life –
you never know, you too might see your wise words in print one day!

www.youaretheauthor.com

People need people

anon@youaretheauthor.com

Strangers are just friends waiting to happen

Be open to the possibility of
forming friendships, even when
you least expect to.

splodge_20@hotmail.com

Love deeply and passionately…

…you might get hurt but it's the only way to live life completely

Don't settle for being an average person — each of us is extraordinary.

Abi37@hotmail.com

I am still an individual when I am with someone

anon@youaretheauthor.com

No one is easy
to live with all
of the time

anon@youaretheauthor.com

Go with the flow

anon@youaretheauthor.com

Remember to put you first

anon@youaretheauthor.com

I am free to go,
so I stay

anon@youaretheauthor.com

Friends may come
and go, but
enemies
accumulate

anon@youaretheauthor.com

Don't let a little dispute injure a great friendship

Pride can easily blow small
matters out of all proportion. Get
some perspective and remember
what's important.

chtann@cheerful.com

Patience is never more important…

…than when you are on the verge of losing it

Try to be aware of your mood changing and your patience slipping – it could save you from saying something you regret.

anon@youaretheauthor.com

The best cure
for a short temper
is a long walk

anon@youaretheauthor.com

Anyone who doesn't think there are two sides to an argument...

...is probably in one

anon@youaretheauthor.com

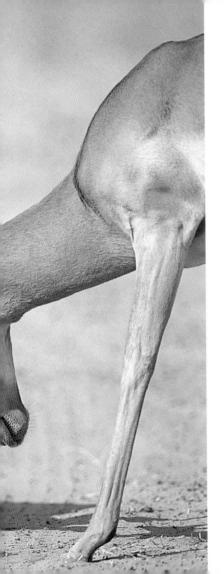

A fight is a
great way to
clear the air

anon@youaretheauthor.com

A loving atmosphere is so important – do all you can to create a tranquil, harmonious home

I try to think of the things I
missed in my home, and make sure
they are there for my kids.

brandon_top@musician.org

Love is unconditional

anon@youaretheauthor.com

Your family is your rock

anon@youaretheauthor.com

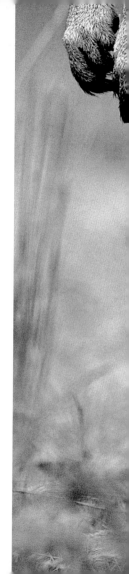

All things
grow with love

anon@youaretheauthor.com

God could not be
everywhere – therefore
he made mothers

So remember her birthday!

anon@youaretheauthor.com

Share your knowledge with your children – it's one way to achieve immortality

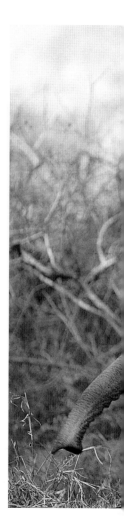

anon@youaretheauthor.com

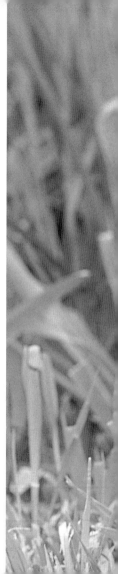

Kids are naturally curious

Weren't you? So don't get angry if
accidents result, it's all in
innocence.

anon@youaretheauthor.com

Let kids be kids

And don't punish them for it,
they only get one chance.

anon@youaretheauthor.com

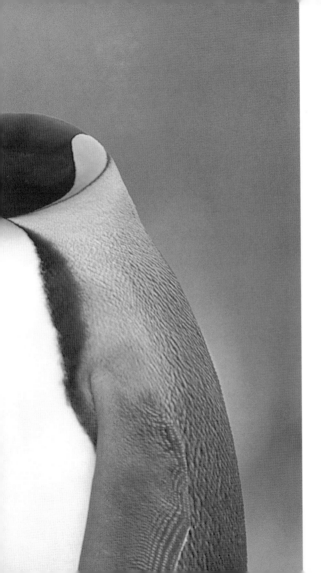

Don't judge
people
by their
relatives

anon@youaretheauthor.com

The most important relationship
in my life is the one with myself

anon@youaretheauthor.com

Better to ask the way than go astray

anon@youaretheauthor.com

The art of good leadership is to consider everyone's opinion but to make up your own mind

Everyone has an opinion, but you have to make the final decision.

anon@youaretheauthor.com

Look at how far you've come, not
at how far you still have to go

anon@youaretheauthor.com

Distance clarifies
everything

anon@youaretheauthor.com

It's alright letting yourself go, as long as you can get yourself back

anon@youaretheauthor.com

Once a year, go someplace you've never been before

Open your arms to change, but don't let go of your values

Being flexible and taking opportunities when they come your way isn't the same as being mercenary with your principles.

suphetty76@hotmail.com

Negative thoughts are a waste of precious energy

Don't undermine yourself – it's hard enough trying to be happy, even when your mind is on your side.

win_vert@paris.com

Nothing is ever as good or as bad as it may seem

Most things don't matter that much in
the long term, so chill out a bit!

anon@youaretheauthor.com

Whether you think you can, or you think you can't…

…you'll be right both ways

Self-belief is all that really matters –
you can do it if you want to.

anon@youaretheauthor.com

Don't be afraid of adversity – you may well be surprised by what you can do

It's OK to come up against obstacles. It is only by rising to a challenge that you find out what you are capable of.

anon@youaretheauthor.com

Good judgment
comes from bad
experiences…

…and a lot of
those are caused
by bad judgment

Life is a learning process, and you can
never be right all the time.

anon@youaretheauthor.com

Experience is a wonderful thing…

…it enables you to recognize a mistake when you make it again

I don't always learn from my mistakes, but I try not to let this get me down!

anon@youaretheauthor.com

No one is good at everything, but everyone is good at something

If you've got kids, make sure they know what it is that they do well, and help bring out these skills.

anon@youaretheauthor.com

Let your
virtues speak
for themselves

Very important for your well-being I think –
walk the walk, don't just talk the talk.

terri.racer@lycos.com

Let people feel the weight of who you are, and let them deal with it

A man is successful if he gets up in the morning…

…goes to bed at night, and in between does what he wants to do

We should all be free to do what most inspires us and feel good about living that way.

Go easy on yourself – you can only take so much

It's foolish to drive yourself to an early grave working too hard – remember to enjoy life as you travel through it.

anon@youaretheauthor.com

A snooze button is a poor substitute for no alarm clock at all

If I have the option, I sleep.

anon@youaretheauthor.com

The early bird gets the worm, but the second mouse gets the cheese

Sometimes there are good reasons not to blindly rush in, but let others lead the way instead.

anon@youaretheauthor.com

Slow and steady
wins the race

anon@youaretheauthor.com

The other line always
moves faster until you join it

anon@youaretheauthor.com

Everything comes
to those who wait

anon@youaretheauthor.com

Kings and their
realms pass away,
but time goes
on forever

anon@youaretheauthor.com

Every moment in time contains the seeds of happiness

I've learned that I can screw up the good times in my life if I'm not focused on the right things, being true to myself and enjoying without strings attached.

anon@youaretheauthor.com

Lead me not into temptation
(I can find the way myself)

anon@youaretheauthor.com

The end of one thing is merely the beginning of another

anon@youaretheauthor.com

Worrying never
changed anything

anon@youaretheauthor.com

When a pessimist has nothing to worry about…

…he worries about why he has nothing to worry about

Don't get into a negative mind-set – enjoy a happy, worry-free period while it lasts.

anon@youaretheauthor.com

Snap out of it, and pull yourself together

Sometimes I just have to remember
this and it gets me motivated again.

anon@youaretheauthor.com

Cheer up! Remember, the less you have, the more there is to get

I get depressed when I look at things in a negative way.

anon@youaretheauthor.com

Fear always springs from ignorance

I try to remember that I am mostly afraid of the situations I am most ignorant of, so there's an easy solution – learn!

rog211us@yahoo.com

If you can stay calm, while all around you is chaos…

…then you probably haven't completely understood the seriousness of the situation

Sometimes it is better to stand back from a difficult situation and not take it too seriously. You are far more likely to find a solution this way than going into a panic.

mariollah@yahoo.com

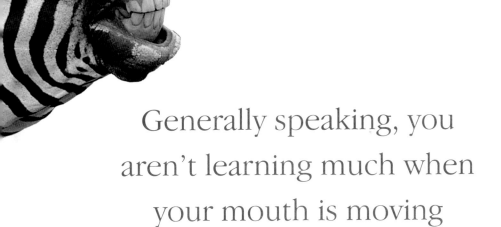

Generally speaking, you aren't learning much when your mouth is moving

Unless you're learning a language.
Otherwise, try to listen a bit more.

mike_pritch20@yahoo.co.uk

Wonder is the beginning of wisdom

anon@youaretheauthor.com

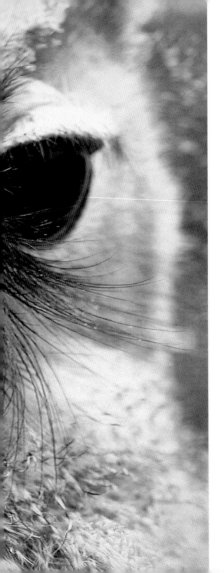

True wisdom is
to live in the present,
plan for the future, and
profit from the past

Imagination is stronger than knowledge…

…dreams are more powerful than facts, and hope can triumph over experience

Whatever setbacks you encounter, don't give up on your hopes and dreams.

toni_agh@in-box.net

Faith begins where reason ends

We reach a point where it's not enough to know something, we have to be willing to step out in faith and start our real journey.

Listen to the silence

anon@youaretheauthor.com

Life – it's nothing like the brochure

anon@youaretheauthor.com